Dearest Barclay!
Friend, brother
and inspiration.
Love Only
Sahana

WELCOME SELF

SURVIVING AND THRIVING
AS A HUMAN BEING

Offered by Lahana Grey

 FriesenPress

Suite 300 - 990 Fort St
Victoria, BC, V8V 3K2
Canada

www.friesenpress.com

Copyright © 2020 by Lahana Grey
First Edition — 2020

Also available in eBook format.

ISBN
978-1-5255-7176-3 (Hardcover)
978-1-5255-7177-0 (Paperback)
978-1-5255-7178-7 (eBook)

1. BODY, MIND & SPIRIT, INSPIRATION & PERSONAL GROWTH

Distributed to the trade by The Ingram Book Company

"A joyous self-discovery. It makes you want to run out and live."

Book sellers, White Dwarf & Dead Write Books

DEDICATION

For my two beautiful daughters, who have been my great teachers and truest friends, always backing me in my adventures even when they had their doubts as to the wisdom of them.

To my grandsons, who have given me the renewed experience of witnessing the growing of wild and unique beings.

BEGINNINGS

Last spring, I travelled to the south of
France with my daughter, her partner,
and her son. An engagement ceremony
was in the works for them with all
kinds of adventures added on.

While there, a fishing trip was set up
for me and my grandson's pleasure. He
loves to fish; I like the release part.

As we cruised the Mediterranean along
the limestone cliffs of the Calanques, I
felt a surge of creativity pierce my heart.
The art that has been still for a few
years rose alive and active in me again.
I was awed and humbled just feeling
the flow of energy, the current within.

On day four, while grabbing a few hours to myself, I tripped on a three-inch step, and to my horror, fell and broke my ankle.

I was trapped in my tiny hotel room, up five flights of stairs with no elevator. I leave it to your imagination as to how I got up there, but let's just say my butt took the brunt of it.

In a room with one window and the view of one tree, shared with my twelve-year-old, tech-crazed grandson, I missed exploring Cassis. It was not easy for us all, but we found a way to be family in it.

Don't worry, the gang brought me food.

The rest of the trip to Toulouse took place with the use of crutches and a wheelchair. Some fun times ensued, and videos were taken of me being shoved around cobblestone lanes, race-track style. I looked ancient, bundled up like a stuffed doll.

The engagement was beautiful with bowers of flowers surrounding the couple and their son. With their commitment spoken and shared, their family was born.

I was home for a few months when I felt this huge pull inside to return to Cassis. It was as if a cord connecting me there yanked me forward towards her. I yielded to the thrilling pull and arranged for an apartment in the heart of Cassis for a month.

Surrendering to the unknown, I was taken...

Not sure when the "writing" will start,
but I sit in the middle of town, a warm
breeze surrounding me, with the scent
of lily of the valley and jasmine that was
sprayed on me by the local perfumer.

I am overwhelmed by the perfection
of landing, being called here.

Market day and purchasing fresh
greens, baguettes, olive oil, and
cheeses. How very French! Oh yeah, a
variety of olives and a pot of basil.

While the apartment is perfect and silent,
I find the urge to be in the human swarm,
so I sit as the market unfolds itself.

As I walk about, I get myself misdirected
many times, so I walk, climb, and
eventually find my bearings.

Home sweating, hot but able,
with a few breaks.

I love being in the town with its
variety, smells, colours, and sounds.

Great to market shop again.
The casual contacts and small
communications, familiar and new.

Welcome Self.

in all your varieties, yet the same.

Welcome Self. As I smile, you smile.

As I offer, so do you.

Response to openness. Gifts of
joy seen and responded to.

Welcome Self.

Writing so familiar. Holding a pen,
it flows without thought, just hand
and movement, like a paintbrush.

Automatic after the first
stroke. I had forgotten.

Welcome Self.

An awakening of movement, known
and unknowable in the action.

Amazing how the church bells chiming
every half hour and marking each hour
is now a comfortable and a reassuring
sound. Two days and I land.

This is a magic place and I settle.

Welcome Self.

I find a patch of sun. Though the shade
is blessedly cool, it is the touch of gold
in the sea breeze that caresses.

Welcome Self.

So what does it mean,

"Welcome Self"?

It is founded in the

"All That Is".

Some call it God, Life Force, Presence,
Energy, or the Vibration of the Universe.

Known and Unknown

Remembered and Forgotten

Loud and in Whispers

Heard and Not

In the "All That Is" is ALL.

All experience, all thought, all birth,
all death, all formed and unformed, all
feelings and all expressions forever
unfolding in the circle of experience. All
time and space is held in the "All That Is".

Nothing is outside of the "All That Is".

And so we come to Love.

Life is passionately in love with itself.

And while some parts of life
forget or deny that truth,

Life does not.

Life seeks to explore all parts of its
experience, remembering that which
has been forgotten and luxuriating
in those parts remembered.

From the "All That Is",

all of Itself is precious.

In our experience, much is
forgotten or called "Other".

How to know oneself?

By feeling and by saying,

"Welcome Self,

You are Me."

Pain, suffering, confusion, and loss
are the results of not knowing or
denying parts of ourselves.

How do we find these?

First, we skip the "why" part of the
questing. That takes us down the
path of multiple answers that are

never ending.

We feel. Recognize the feeling
and, if possible, the trigger that
brought up the feeling.

But the trigger is not necessary.

Then we "Welcome Self".

Just own it; just say it. 'Tis a part,
that for whatever reason, has been

denied, forgotten, or in its imagined
protection of itself, called "Other".

Freedom is the ownership
of all aspects of self.

Welcome Self.

Forgotten Parts.

It is not always the "kick in the gut" or
"screaming voice of denial", but more
often the slight unease or wiggly sensation
that causes an unsettled feeling.

A response to a seen or overheard
event that takes us by surprise.

They are aspects that are oh so subtle,
yet still there. Even if they are on
the outskirts of our awareness, they
still need to be fully absorbed.

Welcome Self.

Often there are parts that have
been observed and felt,

but not yet wholeheartedly owned.

Ahh, those subtle bits hiding in their
simplicity, tucking into corners,
trying to be oh so unobtrusive.

The Tricky Bits.

The wonderful thing about this process of
healing and expansion is that you don't need
to know how or where the forgetfulness
started. It's just the human journey.

Drop the "why".

Just feel, and if insights show up,
then wonderful. The personality
is equally satisfied.

The swift way to ease and peace is
through the action of Welcoming Self.

Your Self, your core of love expands through
the welcoming of its pushed-aside aspects.

How precious to bring home all the
forgotten and denied parts.

Welcome you dear, dear Self.

Imagine being that Centre bringing
home and naming all as Self.

No others, just One integrated.

The weaving complete.

Nothing is outside of the "All That Is".

Some may say, "I have never. This is not
me, for I wouldn't. I don't remember,
yet I feel a twinge deep inside."

The response is the clue. If there is no
feeling but acceptance, then that aspect
is nestled within and held as treasure.

The feeling that rejects and calls it "Other"
is the clue to an unintegrated, unseen,
unknown, and forgotten part of ourself.

Response is:

"Welcome Self."

In that moment of claiming,

the heart quickens,

for Self is expanded and
rejoices at the Reunion.

To Know is to Love.

To Love is to Know.

Acceptance is Freedom

From anguish

From suffering

From doubt

From despair

From depression.

I accept, I welcome my Beloved Self.

Friday Market.

A man walks by, and I think he
has a squirrel on his head.

It is a giant, fuzzy man bun.

It must be a local woman. She is in
high heels. With no fear of falling
on the cobblestone walkways,
she trots confidently on.

Families trying to catch their runaway
kids. I gaze at babies and smile with
their parents. Same everywhere.

So many smoke. I see the thoughts and opinions of smoking arise. I hold her.

Welcome Self.

The joy of being with the family here.

I love the crowds and all the beautiful spots to sit and observe life.

I awake in the night, surprise, with insights around awareness.

Being self-aware. Aware of Self.

An image of a turtle on a long beach with hills in the background.

Seeing only where its head can
swing, so most is unseen.

Then the shell begins to crack enough that
it is going to fall apart, leaving the turtle
exposed. How scary for the turtle and yet
so liberating for it to feel the wind and
sun upon its being. It could be attacked; it
could be seen as it is without its armour.

Welcome Self.

So too ourselves, in truth exposed and
vulnerable when the imaginings or
cloaking of the familiar Self get expanded
by welcoming the not familiar.

How am I that? I thought it was
outside – Other. What?!

It is me? This mess? This hurt that is
causeless or has a perceived cause?

Welcome Self.

Ahh, I forgot you. How precious
you are. You did this or that?

So what? The pain we've held
towards ourselves is done.

Welcome Self.

You forgot that there was nothing
you could do that could stop me from
welcoming you into my Love.

It's not even about forgiveness.

For in your innocence, you forgot,
and so I remember for you.

Back to turtle.

We really do run about holding covers
over us, as the fear of being seen
as we are is terrifying. Our dark
areas. Visions of unbearable actions
that shame and frighten us.

It must be another.

I am not selfish.

I am not violent.

I am not judgmental.

It has to be the Other.

But what if it is? Could it be we hid those
parts under the shell of forgetfulness?

What if we Welcome All Parts
of our humanity as Self?

How exquisite. How delicious to
feel and know all as Self.

Welcome Self.

Welcome Home.

Welcome my Beloved.

Today, after a wonderful sleep, I had a
very slow-moving morning. Feeling fresh,
I think I will stay in and maybe head
out for supper later. The plans change.
By noon, I am out wandering about.

Lunch in a tiny café, and I find the
first white wine I like. What a treat.

How is it that in a lane, there are two
restaurants side by side, with similar
tables, awnings, and candles on their
tables, yet one is filled with folks laughing
and eating and the other is empty?

I watch, and the men in the empty
café stand and watch the people
as they read the menu.

No connection, no hello, no welcome.

They wait, ovens ready, food
prepped. No one enters.

The one that is full is welcoming, whether folks stay or not, they are still welcomed.

The other so sad, empty, wondering, confused.

Welcome you dear, dear Self.

Now for the illusion of the onion.

Layer upon layer, each with a different story. Stories while fodder for the mind can also be changed at the whim of the same mind.

Look, see, discover another story, another layer, and look at the juicy details. Another part to play with, and yes, ultimately integrate.

Oh, but the time it takes to wander back through the paths of previous tales, details and follies endless.

How about another way that is swifter and easier, though not without feeling?

Time is not linear.

For us here to relate, connect,
and share life, it appears so.

The wonder is that all time
is happening now!

Ahh, just observe the clock is round.

The Divine Light, Higher Self, Conscious Self,
or Discovered Awareness is the Centre-post.

All around the centre, as if numbers on a
clock, are our life experiences, happening
in the life that is being lived now.

Everything is Now.

Even lives that have been journeyed in
other times, if yet to be fully known, if
unseen as Self, will brilliantly show up in
this life to be recognized and experienced.

As life demands to be known, it will
find a way to enter and show itself.

We access these times through feeling.

When a feeling of stuck-ness, pain,
judgment, or any other awareness arises
and presents itself, we observe our
Self. Our resistance or unwillingness
to Welcome Self is the clue.

Hello, dear one, my precious part that
I forgot and turned my back on.

I see you. Come in, come
home, you belong as Me.

Welcome precious. Let yourself join
and offer your journey to the whole.

You belong, my love.

There is nothing you could do, believe,
or hide from that I don't love.

Welcome Self.

Your experiences enrich Me
and our human journey.

I would not be whole without you,

my Self.

Back to the onion and its layers, which
is readily accepted in our current belief
system, yet also entails work.

(We have to work hard to heal.)

What if, just instead, we had awareness
and accepted that our whole experience
as it is, is happening now?

All is accessible by following the feeling.
When it is felt and truly welcomed
unconditionally, as the Mother/
Father does to its child, it is Love.

Are we not that?

So simple, so easy to

Welcome Self.

And yes, sometimes the mind seems so powerful as it tries to steer us back into the chatter. We observe the mind and say, "I see you." Mind ceases by our commitment to be in the moment, in the "what is".

Dear Self, I hold you, I know you,
you belong in Me as Me.

Welcoming as Self

beauty, wonder, birthing, passing,
doubt, pain, loss, darkness, light,
day, night, radiance, scents,
flowering, changing, seasons, cold,
warm, plants, and all creatures,

so treasured~so glorious, so
belonging, so fitting.

No part left behind

No part left unknown

No part left unloved

Every part blended into the whole.

Vibrating in the Resonance of Love.

And in case you haven't noticed,

This is a Love Story

Belonging To Us All.

Turtles, clocks, and other inspirations.

Today, wind and cooler weather.
A treat for me, but how it relates
except for comfort, I don't know.

There is an ease that gives the being
an experience devoid of stress.

Arrive spider.

Programmed stress, caused by accumulated
stories making freeways in the brain that
can trigger a plethora of emotions.

Multiple tales that appear too confusing
to disseminate or take apart.

Rather than trying to separate the knot
or tease the threads apart, just welcome
Self in all your tangled confusion.

It could be lifetimes. Attempting to find each
story and unravel them all will take the same
amount of time that it did to create them.

Instead, welcome Self to all our
messy, tangled, woven thoughts
and perceived experiences.

Even a hardball is made up of hundreds
of feet of thread woven tightly around
a core. Knowing or not knowing
the make-up of each thread doesn't
change the feel in one's hand.

Welcome Self.

I hold you in your totality.

Indeed always, in the unclear, the
foggy, the tightness of binding,

I hold you.

How great not to have to know it all.

How wonderful not to need
to understand, just~

Welcome Self.

I hold you.

I know you.

And I love you as you are.

Market day. So active, alive, and
moving at an easy pace.

And so today welcomes snail.

As I leave the apartment, a huge
snail finds its way along the walkway
with its house upon its back.

I wonder at its message as I say,

"Welcome Self."

But now, as I reflect on the
market and the ease of flow,

I feel her

winding her way, her slow movement,
and in her ease, she sees all.

Time slows in a way to absorb;
all senses alive and awake.

Parts of life that would otherwise be
missed are recognized and touched.

Welcome Self.

So I emulate snail and see and feel more.

The days move on, as they will. The
leaves above, while not ready to fly
away, are losing their subtleness and
starting to dry. The breeze has a coolness
that is offset by the sun as it rises.

Fall finds its way in with nary a
whisper of frost. Days and nights
in equal balance. Delicious.

Welcome Self.

After the day in the small cafés on the
side streets, markets, and laneways, I
find my way to a harbour-side café.

Filtered by the leaves that shelter the
tables, it is quiet and peaceful.

Welcome Self.

Is there any occasion when "Welcome Self" is not applicable?

It appears not.

For challenges, "Welcome Self" aids in the absorption and acceptance of that particular aspect.

Gratitude swells when the Self is recognized and held.

The heart is full.

Saturday in Cassis. The town is swarming, as it is the one day when all the stores are having huge sales.

Packed! A wonderful feeling with music in the air, played by a street musician at the harbour.

Overwhelmed with love and joy
by just being in Family.

Am surrounded by French, the familiar,
but barely understandable tongue.

A blur of sounds, laughter, and general
holiday atmosphere permeates all.

Welcome Self.

Today I awoke, oh yippee, and enjoyed
the simple tasks of hand-washing
my lacy bits and hanging them to
dry, tidying the kitchen, etc.

Decided to do a walkabout. The sidewalk
sale is still on, same musician playing,
but less folks. Somehow it had lost its
charm. I had changed. Wandered.

Welcome Self.

Lunch at David's, which was delicious but
felt somewhat unsettled as if the colours

had faded. Everyone as open and friendly, but I felt like a specter floating though.

Welcome Self.

Home and a nap. Hardly ever napped before here. Very soothing.

A cruise ship on the horizon and memories flood. Doubts arise as to the writing.

Welcome Self.

I love you and follow

You, Beloved.

The wind howled all night; trees being tossed, branches banging on the walls, tangled in themselves, twisting and catching. Roots and trunks strong, while their branches surrendered to movement that was out of their control.

No thought whether to surrender
or not. Just being swept as the
wind moves them, taking over.

Such are our lives. As life has its way with
us, we only pretend that we have control. Or
judge ourselves. Saying, "If only I had done
this or that, things would be different."

Ahh, poor dear Self, still in the illusion of
power and choice. Forgetting that the Grace,
Life, wants to know itself in its totality. So
here Love, remember this? Remember that?

'Tis you.

Welcome Self.

No resistance to feelings.

Avoidance is the clue.

If we avoid, skim, or skirt over a feeling,
that is where we need to start. If we

scurry away from those feelings, no
matter how subtle, they become HABIT.

Often so strong, even with all
our reassuring explanations as to
"why", it is barely seen or felt.

Avoidance.

Allow the wind of desire to move into
the cracks – and there always are
cracks – to tease and brush inward
till it gains full purchase. Ahh, finally
exposed. All we protected was based in
the illusion of our awful or guilty Self.

Welcome Self.

You hid from Me, not knowing I don't
care what shame or doubts you had
tucked away. I love you. I accept
you. And you are seen as human.

Welcome Self.

It becomes an adventure to observe
and feel our habits and discover
another part that is hiding.

Ahh, my love~ welcome.

The last few days, I have observed my habit
of being moved by time, as it is here.

The feeling of being on time, following
the timed events around me, and
generally adhering to them.

Here in this town so far away from
my routines, I have been consciously
attempting to live in a rhythm away from
time. Following my own inner impelling.

The humour in that is there are church bells
that sound 24 hours a day, marking the

hour with the same number of bells as the
hour and with one bell on the half hour.

So the demand that we know
the time is never ending

But over time, ha-ha.

The sound becomes vibrations cast out
as far as the waves will push them.

I still on occasion count the number
of bells equalling time. The pressure
to know time is calming.

Imagine enough time for all things.
Eat, sleep, work, all movements from
within. Mind you, I am on holiday
with no one to answer to.

No children off to school, to be
fed, to be listened to and played
with while fitting in work.

That is another time that Life makes
happen as well. Once again Life
has its way! Welcome Self.

The pressure eases, and I flow. I feel
easier in this life with time flowing
through knowing it has its own wisdom.

Welcome Self.

Anyone who knows me will know this is
a big deal, for I'm always on time, if not
early. Deep down, I felt if I were late, time
would whop me good. So time let me go.
I let you go, knowing you too belong.

Time is part of the intelligence
that orchestrates the show, having
its own flow and purpose.

Welcome Self.

The beauty of this way or process is
that it can be used by all, no matter
what your tradition – path or no path.

The knowing of yourself as Self is
unlimited and all inclusive.

Though any tradition that feels it's the only one has an opportunity for growth as it sees itself and all others, in the "All That Is".

Any perceived one way that feels its exclusivity will be humbled as it stumbles into love for the whole of ourselves.

When it is said that all aspects are in the "All That Is", that is the truth. Hence, the light of acceptance is shone on the whole of Humanity.

Every part a fragment of the "All That Is", desiring to be known.

Love then has its way with all that is revealed.

Welcome Self.

Last night, I awoke with the seeing and
feeling of a great black bear tethered by a
long rope that was staked into the ground.

I went up and loosened the ties
so that it could be free.

Who is black bear for us now?

He was a performer. And so we face
that part that is a performer.

Some parts of the performer we play and
dance with, but there are other parts of the
performer that cover who we really are.

Let's look at picture taking. Mostly
we pose wanting the best view of
ourselves to be captured and seen.
How often do we just throw caution to
the wind and show all of our Self?

Fun one, crazy one, beautiful one,
angry one, fearful one in fresh
unselfconsciousness. Even the parts
we don't like. Hiding them deep not to
be seen as we try to project another

view. And we say try, because the
wholeness demands to be seen.

Can we continue performing certain roles
knowing it is only a part of ourselves?

Time to be real in all our glory,
ugliness, and messiness.

Welcome Self.

What would happen if we were
exposed? Would we still be loved?

Would we still love ourselves
is the real question.

Time for welcoming the whole Self.

It takes courage to be authentic.
But we are brave~

it is in us.

Humans expand from challenges.

Let's step up with each other and
let our humanness reign.

Acknowledge again and again those actions we deny in ourselves, as we see them played out around us, calling them "Other". Instead, call them our Self.

As we throw out our un-welcomed parts to the humans around us, what if in the knowing we are part of the "All That Is", we instead use our courage and see them as Self? What if in the acceptance of "All That Is" around us, we instead offer kindness to the One Self.

Welcome Self.

There is another part of bear that is tied up, struggling, suffering, and trying to get free from its binds and entrapment. Helpless.

It is a life that is surviving just enough to live. Not enough to expand, to run, to explore the environs around it. Proverbial circle life. Just holding on.

Often it finds commonality
with those around them.

If anger and frustration is the response to
that life, then a group will form, lashing
out, protesting the life they find themselves
in. Always other, and the mind agrees,
providing additional fuel for a movement
toward the perceived cause. Pain ensues.

For others, the situation is so painful
that a crack in the heart can occur as
we cry out for help and change.

It's a universal cry. No matter whether a
Self has a belief or not, an opening has
been created for letting go, surrendering.

In that moment, compassion finds its way
into the being. Grace enters, expanding
the heart, allowing acceptance to rise. In
acceptance, love enters into the life as it is.

Welcome Self.

The life circumstances may change as there
is an opening, a space for the life to expand.

Opportunities can enter. Even if the physical life stays the same, in the peace that flowers within, the cords that bind dissolve.

Freedom as the life, while same
in some ways, is a new experience
that envelops the moment.

Breath flows, tension drops, and
a gratitude for life unfolds.

The "As It Is" emerges itself into
the body, mind, and heart.

Grace flows and compassion unfolds
in the vibration of Love.

Now we thrive.

Welcome Self.

As I see the wind trigger the trees to
dance, they respond to the touch and let
themselves be moved without thought.

And I, so used to the pen flowing
on paper, as I breathe, ask for the
poetry of love and life to enter.

Morning softness, a time of tender light as
the mists are absorbed by the light motes.

Clearer, sharper the landscape's resolution
appears. Like awakening from an amorphous
dream state, I try to hold on to the softness,
and yet the sharpness of the day takes over.

Let me stay in the other worldliness.
The fog of soft potential.

The place of unformed. Unknown desires
filtered in the unconscious, arising as
vague longings and self-wanderings.

Welcome Self.

The finishing of the first writing
has the same feeling as birth and
with a similar aftermath.

Happy for the birth and a little lost as
the emptied body is no longer full.

The mists of desire float about like clouds
who haven't decided whether to gather and
deepen or dissipate at the touch of the sun.

They cannot choose but leave it up
to the winds without effort.

Unsettled Self, I hold you.

This morning I am still unsettled.

Welcome Self.

The vision mostly complete, and
yet and I still feel unfocused.

And so I sit and absorb.

Eat and feel the edginess dissolve as
I allow the just being~ness to flow
in. I welcome the nothingness and in
it the moving purpose dissolves.

Allowing and welcoming the
un~known, un~doing. Using this
time to be a floater, a be~er.

Welcome Self

in the unknown, unknowable bliss.

It always amazes me how literally home
is where you are. About one month
here, and the landscape and feeling of
the place has become a part of me.

Welcome Self.

In the familiar apartment with the stunning
view that shows the same structures,
but in every moment is different.

A moving picture of light, sharpness
and softness, reflectiveness, precision,
dissolving, and always breathtaking.

I leave tomorrow, and while it is the
perfect moment to do so, this Cassis
has embedded itself into my life.

The feeling, the people flowing, always
welcoming now a part of me.

I love you,

my Beloved.

Thank you Self for creating this time of
silence and rest. Hill and step climbing
a bit of an effort but doable. The silence
of an unknown language. The silence
of the village and the castle on the
cliffs. Sea pounding on the shore while
lightning and thunder light the sky
in advance of the exploding rain.

Thank you, love. You always know best.

I love you, Self, in your

"All That Is"~ness!

NOTES

Love Guided ~ She willingly followed

Lahana Grey is a mother, grandmother, friend, poet, painter, and spiritual counsellor. She notes: "Two elements have been a constant compass in my life – creativity and spirituality. Through these forces I fully trust the gifts that flow. I am humbled by the trust life has in me to share truthfully."

Now being what she terms as "vintage", Lahana has lots of time to live her dreams as they land upon her. She trusts her heart to lead, and in spite of wounds along the way, her spirit has thrived. A traveller and adventurer, she has visited many alluring countries, each with their own set of challenges and victories. Through these journeys, she experienced genuine kinship with the women, men, and children of those lands, as she was welcomed into their lives. These experiences are the everlasting gifts that she treasures every day.

www.welcomeself.ca